Piano·Vocal·Chords

Bruce Hornsby

Hot House

Album Produced on RCA Records
by Bruce Hornsby
Manangement: Q Prime, Inc.
Album Art Direction & Design: Ria Lewerke
and Norman Moore
Cover Illustration: Gary Kelly
Back Cover Photography: William Claxton
All Other Photography: Kathy Hornsby

Book Editor: Sy Feldman

CONTENTS

BIG RUMBLE 88

THE CHANGES 51

COUNTRY DOCTOR 97

CRUISE CONTROL 67

HOT HOUSE BALL 31

THE LONGEST NIGHT 46

SPIDER FINGERS 7

SWING STREET 58

THE TANGO KING 22

WALK IN THE SUN 40

WHITE WHEELED LIMOUSINE 74

SPIDER FINGERS

Words and Music by
B.R. HORNSBY

Ha!

8

10

do the spi - der fin - - gers.___

Check the Spider Fingers!

14

(Additional piano - 2nd time only)

To Coda ⊕

Spider Fingers - 15 - 8
PF9529

D.S. %al Coda

How

...end solo)

E♭ma7/F   F 6   E♭ma7/F   F 6

(Piano solo...

22

THE TANGO KING

Words and Music by
B.R. HORNSBY

Moderately fast Creole rock ♩ = 150

Tango King - 9 - 1
PF9529

2. Here she comes,___ com-ing 'round the bend.__ Been___ to the bath-room and
3. Look at Pete,_____ He's a lounge hand._ All___ want to stand_

go-ing back a-gain.___ Fix the hair,__ ba-by pow-der that shine just_
where he stands.___ Spin that girl__ be-neath the col-ored ball. Fan -

___ to give a good cold_ shoul-der next_ time._____
-cy plaid man's the__ en-vy of__ all._____

Chorus:

28

HOT HOUSE BALL

Words and Music by
B.R. HORNSBY

Hothouse Ball - 9 - 1
PF9529

32

Verse 2:
We can dance in the streets any night or day.
The big ball men built such a nice old park.
One day we'll celebrate every Halloween.
Our faces as masks, everyone glow in the dark.

Chorus 2:
Don't light a match, don't play with fire,
Step real lightly 'round the barbed wire.
Keep the noise down to hear the meltdown call,
Living in the shadow of the hothouse ball.

WALK IN THE SUN

Words and Music by
B.R. HORNSBY

Hmm.

One day, we'll walk in the sun.

Verse:

1. My name is Ver-non James,___ and I live___ to the south of town.___
2. I'm tak-ing tick-ets and watch-ing the men___ al-ways look-ing down.___

Walk in the Sun - 6 - 1
PF9529

Repeat ad lib. and fade

One day, we'll walk in the sun.

One day, we'll walk in the sun.___

THE LONGEST NIGHT

Words and Music by
B.R. HORNSBY

Moderate shuffle feel ♩ = 84

Verses 1 & 2:

1. Some-one's danc-ing on the ta - ble, some-one's got an old book_ in the
2. Most ev-ery-one all a - round,_ most have an in-ter-est-ing

back._ Some old jocks sit-ting 'round their_ neigh-bors, e-ven
sto-ry. E - ven those who don't have much_ to say, e-ven

50

The Longest Night - 5 - 5
PF9529

THE CHANGES

Words and Music by
B.R. HORNSBY

54

Verses 3, 4 & 5:

3. The own - er says__ he thinks we need some work,__ got a
white girl in a da - shi - ki says you're all the rage, my
5. Old friend Dave__ with the sil - ver spoon__ says

55

Changes - 7 - 5
PF9529

56

Repeat as desired for solos

SWING STREET

Words and Music by
B.R. HORNSBY

𝄋 *Verses 2 - 4:*

2. My friend John with a mir-ror and spoon,
3. Nice old man in the cor - ner booth,
4. Cut - ting con - tests on the stand,

62

Chorus:

like a good time, a ball to me,____ sounds like a place I'd like to be.____ There's____ Ev -

____ a lit - tle crowd____ you're gon - na want to meet.____ } Oh, they
- ery - bod - y rolls____ when it's time to meet.____

got a thing go - ing on____ Swing Street.____

Swing Street - 9 - 5
PF9529

64

Swing Street - 9 - 7
PF9529

66

Repeat ad lib. and fade

Swing Street - 9 - 9
PF9529

CRUISE CONTROL

Moderately fast ♩ = 72

Words and Music by
B.R. HORNSBY

Verses 1-2:

1. It's been a long time com - ing___ this feel - ing I've got.___
hold - ing on, he trust - ed me then he slipped a - way.___

Things-'ll al - ways go___ your way,___ such a long shot.___
He fell hard___ and now I've___ just got___ my - self to blame.___

Cruise Control - 7 - 1
PF9529

70

where you go, wheels roll__ and the whis-tle will blow. Man - y miles,_ oh, I_

__ may roam. Put it in drive,_ and set the cruise con - trol.

2. He was cruise con - trol.

72

son.

I could feel it tak - ing me down

_ to stay.___

Then I said,

D.S. 𝄋 al Coda

"For- get this, it's out of your hands an - y - way."___

⊕ *Coda*

4. Oh, where__ I'll go,__ I just__ don't know.__

WHITE WHEELED LIMOUSINE

Words and Music by
B.R. HORNSBY

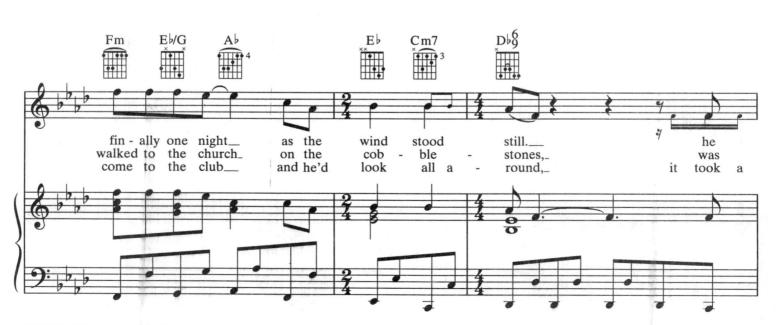

78

White Wheeled Limousine - 14 - 5
PF9529

(Banjo solo)

84

White Wheeled Limousine - 14 - 11
PF9529

85

(Banjo echo)

White Wheeled Limousine - 14 - 12
PF9529

White wheeled lim-ou-sine stand-ing a - lone,___ stand - ing, stand - ing a - lone.__

BIG RUMBLE

Words and Music by
B.R. HORNSBY

Verses 1 & 2:

cocked   and   read - y,   oh___ here   I   stand,   an -
young   girls   scream - ing   as   the   gym   rat   speaks,   might

Big Rumble - 9 - 1
PF9529

89

Big Rumble - 9 - 2
PF9529

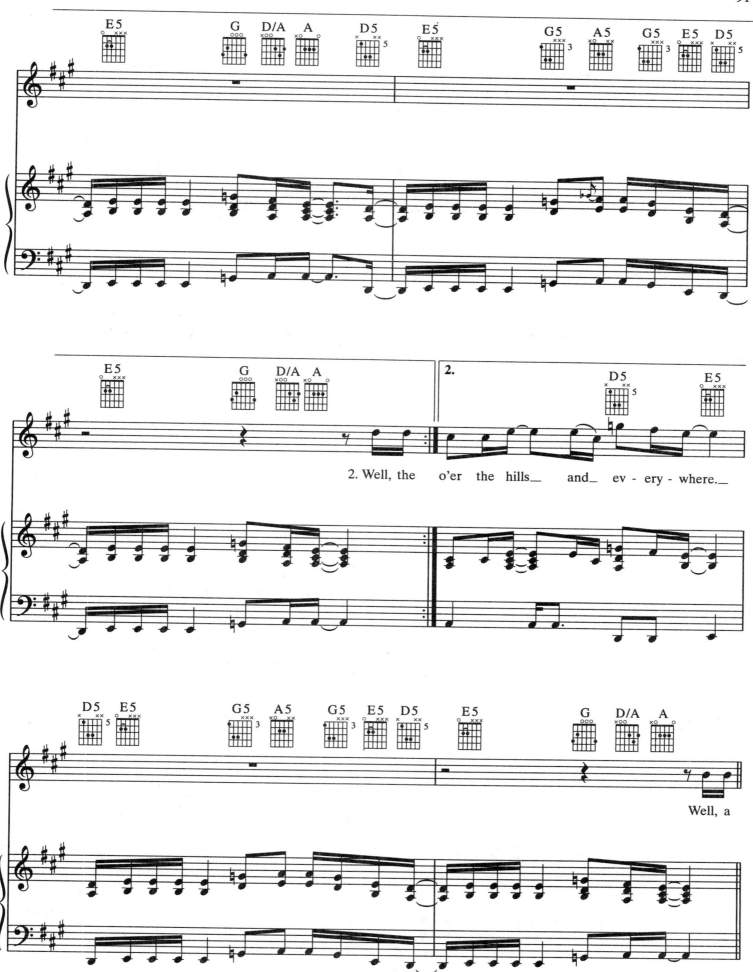

94

Big Rumble - 9 - 7
PF9529

96

Repeat ad lib. and fade

Big Rumble - 9 - 9
PF9529

COUNTRY DOCTOR

Words and Music by
B.R. HORNSBY

Verse:

1. Deep down in the south coun - ty, o-ver where the pa-per mill__ runs,

lived a man, a young coun - try doc - tor with the per - fect wife and sons.

Well, he

...end Gtr. solo

Repeat ad lib. and fade

Verse 2:
My guess, there was another woman.
And with the kids and the money,
There was a lot to lose.
He said she had a rare affliction
And he was doing all he could do.
And we all believed him,
Felt so sorry and then
I thought once he was a fine man.
Now, I don't remember when.

Chorus 2:
I saw the country doctor
To ask him what was wrong with me.
He was caught unaware, accidental and
Devil may care.
Behind the curtain, I see bottles
Unmarked in front of me.
Whoa, nobody knows the trouble I've seen.

Chorus 3:
I saw the country doctor
In a place where he didn't see me.
Way out in the middle of the night
Where he thought no one could see.
Over there in the parlor room,
Making eyes, hands roaming free.
Someone soon must know the trouble
I've seen.